Everyday Food

Bread

Joyce Bentley

Chrysalis Children's Books

First published in the UK in 2005 by
Chrysalis Children's Books
An imprint of Chrysalis Books Group Plc
The Chrysalis Building, Bramley Road, London W10 6SP

ISBN 1 84458 180 2

British Library Cataloguing in Publication Data
for this book is available from the British Library.

Senior editor *Rasha Elsaeed*
Project editor *Debbie Foy*
Editorial assistant *Camilla Lloyd*
Food consultant *Brenda Alden*
Art director *Sarah Goodwin*
Illustrator *Molly Sage*
Designer *Ben Ruocco, Tall Tree Ltd*
Picture researchers *Sarah Stewart-Richardson, Veneta Bullen, Miguel Lamas*

Printed in China

10 9 8 7 6 5 4 3 2 1

Words in **bold** can be found in Words to remember on page 30.

Typography *Natascha Frensch*
Read Regular, READ SMALLCAPS and Read Space; European Community Design Registration 2003
and Copyright © Natascha Frensch 2001-2004 **Read Medium**, **Read Black** and *Read Slanted*
Copyright © Natascha Frensch 2003-2004

READ™ is a revolutionary new typeface that will enhance children's understanding through clear, easily
recognisable character shapes. With its evenly spaced and carefully designed characters, READ™ will help
children at all stages to improve their literacy skills, and is ideal for young readers, reluctant readers and
especially children with dyslexia.

Picture Acknowledgements
All reasonable efforts have been made to ensure the reproduction of content has been done with the consent
of copyright owners. If you are aware of any unintentional omissions please contact the publishers directly so
that any necessary corrections may be made for future editions.

Anthony Blake Photo Library: Maximillian Stock Ltd 4, David Marsden 8L, Amanda Heywood 15T, Sue Atkinson
21T, Martin Brigdale 21B; Chrysalis Image Library: 51 14, Ray Moller 24T, 24B, 25; Corbis: Dave G. Houser 8R,
Shai Ginott 9, Jacqui Hurst 13B, Charles Gupton 15B, Alison Wright 23T, Norbert Schaefer 27B; Federation
of Bakers: BC, 16, 17, 18; Frank Lane Picture Agency: Life Science Images FC, Catherine Mullen 7, Roger
Wilmshurst 10T, 12, Peter Dean 10B, David Hosking 11; Holt Studios: Nick Spurling 19; Powerstock: Nils Johan
Norenlind; Rex Features: United National Photographers 22; Royalty Free: 1, 20, 23B, 26; Werner Forman
Archive: Dr. E. Strouhal 6; Wright's Flour: 13T.

Contents

What is bread?

Bread is a food that we eat. Basic bread is made from flour, **yeast** and water. We can add fat and salt to bread.

There are many types of bread such as white, brown, granary, **wholemeal** and **rye**.

Bread made with yeast is called **leavened** bread as the yeast makes it rise. Bread without yeast is **unleavened** and is flat.

Vikings made holes in their bread so that it could be stored on tent pegs.

Danish pastries have sugar added to the **dough** to make them sweet.

Back in time

Bread making dates back to the Egyptians. In 3000 BC, they began to add yeast to make the bread dough rise. The Romans improved bread making by using better **mills** and ovens.

This ancient Egyptian painting shows people mixing and **kneading** bread dough.

Windmills and water-mills improved flour making. When steam power was invented, flour making became even faster.

In ancient Egypt, bread was so important that people were paid their wages with it.

The Victorians invented the threshing machine to separate the wheat grains from the stalk during **harvesting**.

All sorts of bread

You can make bread using different flours such as brown, white, wholemeal or rye.

Bread comes in many shapes and sizes. These are called rolls.

French bread contains butter and eggs. It is cooked in long rolls called baguettes.

Savoury breads are made with tomato, cheese, olives, seeds, onion or potato. Sweet bread is made with sugar, fruit, nuts or honey.

This woman is making flat, unleavened bread.

Cereals and grains

Cereals are plants that contain **grains**. Flour is made by **grinding** the grains. **Wheat** is the most common cereal used to make flour.

Oats and barley are used to make bread and porridge.

Wheat grains are the golden buds at the top of the plant.

Wheat is planted in fields and when it is fully grown it is harvested. Farmers spray the plants with **fertilisers** to help them grow.

The harvesting machine gathers the wheat and a **thresher** separates the grains from the **stalk**.

Flour and milling

The wheat is dried in a **silo** before going to the mill. At the mill, the outer layer of the grain is removed. The inner part is crushed in between large rollers until it becomes flour.

In the past, windmills were used to turn large stones that ground the wheat into flour.

Today, modern rolling machines grind the wheat into flour.

Brown bread is made from white flour mixed with **bran**, and wholemeal bread uses the whole grain.

The flour is packed into sacks and taken by lorry to the bakery.

Making bread

Flour, yeast, water and salt are mixed into a soft dough. The dough is kneaded so that the yeast will start to make it rise.

The baker has to knead the dough for up to 20 minutes.

If the dough does not prove, the bread will be hard when cooked.

The dough is placed in a warm cupboard or wrapped in cloth and left to **prove**. The warmth allows the yeast to act on the dough.

The dough is baked in a hot oven until it is golden brown.

In the factory

Most of the bread we eat is made in a factory. The dough is made in large containers using electric mixers.

Mixing machines knead the dough by moving it around large **vats**.

Dough is cut into pieces and placed in baking tins where it is allowed to prove. The dough moves along the **conveyor belt** to the ovens for baking.

In the past, the best part of the **loaf** was the 'upper crust'. So rich, important people became known by this name!

When cool, the bread is wrapped ready for selling.

Getting to you

Hundreds of loaves are made every day at the factory. They are packed onto lorries to be delivered to shops and supermarkets around the country.

Bread is packed into crates before being loaded onto lorries.

Some supermarkets bake their own bread. Fresh bread is placed on shelves ready for customers to buy.

You can buy all kinds of loaves, rolls, **croissants** and cakes at the supermarket.

Eating bread

Most people eat bread every day. We can eat bread on its own, with soup or use it to make sandwiches.

The sandwich was named after the Earl of Sandwich who was too busy to eat a proper meal.

You can toast
bread, cover it with
toppings or use it
to make desserts.

Sandwiches
are an ideal
meal to take
to school in
a lunchbox.

Bread-and-butter
pudding is made
with milk, eggs,
sugar and raisins.

Everyone loves bread

Bread is the **staple diet** of many people around the world. Wheat is plentiful, cheap and bread is easy to bake.

Jewish unleavened bread is eaten during **Passover**.

Bread is used in many festivals and ceremonies and each country has its own special bread recipe.

Naan is a flat, white bread that is baked in a hot, clay oven.

Bread rolls filled with burgers, salad and sauces are a popular meal.

A balanced diet

Bread is a **carbohydrate**. It also contains **fibre** and **vitamins**. We need these nutrients as part of a balanced diet.

Common carbohydrates are potatoes, rice and pasta.

Fruit and vegetables contain carbohydrates and provide lots of vitamins and fibre.

For a balanced diet, most of the food we eat should come from the groups at the bottom of the chart and less from the top.

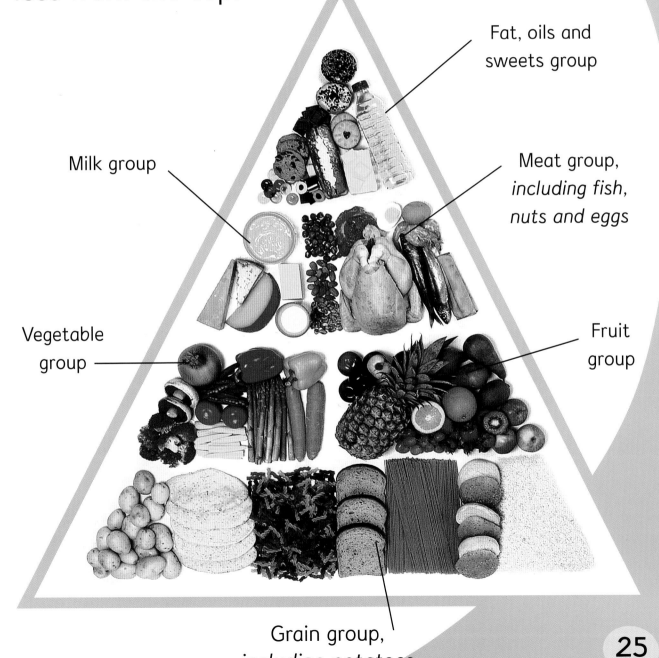

Fat, oils and sweets group

Milk group

Meat group, *including fish, nuts and eggs*

Vegetable group

Fruit group

Grain group, *including potatoes*

Healthy bread

We need carbohydrates to give us energy and fibre to help our **digestion**. Wholemeal bread is good as it contains lots of fibre.

Children need carbohydrates to be active.

Athletes eat carbohydrates when they are training to give them more energy.

Minerals, such as iron and calcium, are added to flour to keep our bones, teeth and blood healthy.

Fibre helps us to digest our food and stops us feeling tired.

Fresh bread rolls

The smell of these freshly cooked bread rolls is delicious! Makes 12 rolls

Children in the kitchen must be supervised at all times by an adult.

YOU WILL NEED

- 450g/1 lb strong bread flour
- 15g/½ oz softened butter
- 1 teaspoon salt
- 1 sachet fast-action dried yeast
- 300 ml/10 fl oz lukewarm water

1. Preheat the oven to 220°C/ 450°F /gas mark 8. Sieve the flour and salt into a bowl and stir in the dried yeast.

2. Add the butter in small chunks. Rub the butter and flour between your fingers until the mixture is crumbly.

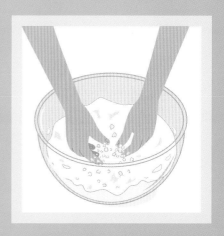

3. Add the water slowly to form the dough into a ball. Knead the dough for 10 minutes.

4. Shape it into 12 small rolls. Leave the rolls in a warm place to prove for about 25 minutes.

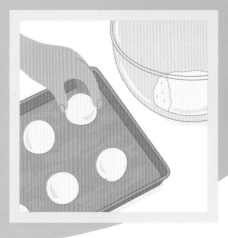

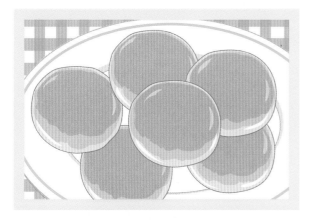

5. Bake for about 15 to 20 minutes on a greased baking tray.

Words to remember

bran The outer layer of the grain that is removed during milling.

carbohydrate Nutrient the body needs for energy.

cereal Grasses that produce edible seeds called grains.

conveyor belt Machine that carries things along.

croissants Breakfast pastries made with butter.

digestion How the body processes food.

dough A soft mixture of flour and water.

fertiliser A substance added to soil to help plants grow.

fibre Material found in plants and grains that helps digestion.

grains The seeds of a cereal plant such as wheat.

grinding To rub something until it becomes like a powder.

harvesting To pull crops from the ground when they are ready to eat.

kneading To squeeze and press dough to spread the yeast.

loaf Bread that is shaped and baked in one piece.

leavened Bread made with yeast to help it rise.

mill A place where grains are ground to make flour.

minerals Nutrients the body needs for good health and to prevent illness.

Passover A Jewish festival.

prove To allow bread dough to rise before cooking.

rye A type of cereal that is used to make flour.

silo A place where wheat is stored to dry.

stalk The upright part of a plant.

staple diet Food that forms the main part of the diet.

thresher A machine that separates the grain from the stalk.

unleavened Bread made without yeast.

vats Large containers used in factories.

vitamins Nutrients the body needs for good health and to prevent illness.

wheat A type of cereal plant.

wholemeal Bread made from flour that uses the inner and outer parts of the grain.

yeast A substance that causes dough to rise when heated.

Index